WELCOME TO WASHINGTON!

Washington, DC, the nation's capital, is best known for its monuments, museums, and galleries—beyond being the seat of the smoke and mirrors of government. What is less appreciated by the millions of visitors who descend upon the city and its environs each year is the outdoor displays of art, murals and graffiti, not unlike that found in many of the world's major cities.

I've lived in the Washington area off and on since 1982, when I retired from the U.S. Army and joined the U.S. Foreign Service. From the beginning, I'd noticed the graffiti, mostly that on walls and bridge abutments along the Washington Metrorail route, but had honestly paid it little attention. Then, in 2014, I was asked to conduct a workshop on professional writing for Rangel Foreign Affairs Fellowship Scholars. This summer program, designed to introduce select college seniors to foreign affairs, is held each June and July at Howard University's Ralph Bunche Center for International Affairs. Because of the paucity of parking in the area, I commuted by Metro twice a week, taking the Red Line from Shadow Grove Station in Gaithersburg to Gallery Place/Chinatown, and changing to the Yellow or Green Line to Shaw/Howard University Station. From the metro station, I walked up Seventh Street to Howard, and along the way, I began to notice the number of murals on building walls and in parking lots, and graffiti, some of it quite artistic, on walls, doors, windows, newspaper bins, and other flat surfaces.

Along with my lecture notes, I carried, as is my habit, a notebook in which to record observations for my books, and my camera for the occasional urban scene to photograph. I began taking pictures of some of the more interesting pieces of street art. After that summer, I began to pay more attention as I traveled around the metro area, and noticed that such art could be found in a great number of places. I began to make a photographic record.

Recently, while walking from a restaurant near the Capitol, toward the metro station at Union Station, I noticed a wall mural near a former homeless shelter. A tourist couple were walking past, and paid it no notice. Something made me stop and snap the photo before they were out of the frame. I then went on my way, but that picture stayed in my mind. It struck me that this couple, interested no doubt in the city's culture, had completely ignored one of its most fascinating elements.

As with most of my ideas for books, this one started as a random event, of no particular consequence, until the following week, during a conversation with Mia Olufemi, an associate producer at WETA, a Washington-area-based PBS station, I discovered that she, too, was fascinated by DC's street art. That conversation solidified the idea to do a book introducing this artistic genre to a broader audience.

What you'll find here is not a museum-level display of street art. It's not even the tip of the iceberg. What it is, is a teaser. A small sampling of what's available—sort of like the food samples you get at places like Costco—designed to whet your appetite to try more.

And, I hope that's exactly what you'll do. If you live in or near the area, the next time you're out and about, look around. I promise you, you'll be pleased and surprised. If you only come on annual trips, add areas like Shaw and the Sixteenth Street corridor in Cardoza (among the many areas that host street art) to your itinerary. You'll go back home with some interesting stories, and maybe even photos, that your friends who didn't read this book won't have.

If, by chance, you happen to like this book, I would also ask that you take a few minutes and leave a review on Amazon, Goodreads, or whatever book site you purchased it from. Reviews are important to independent authors to get the word out, so even a few words will do.

Happy reading, happy viewing, and who knows, I might just run into you around town as I further document DC's street art.

DC Street Art

Murals and Graffiti in and around the Nation's Capital

Charles Ray

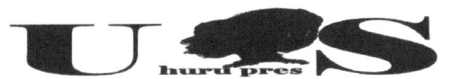

Uhuru Press

North Potomac, MD

The photographs contained in this book are the intellectual property of the author/photographer. Reproduction or distribution by any means, print or electronic, without the express written permission of the author/photographer is a violation of copyright law.

For information about this or other works by this author, contact him at

harlesray.author@gmail.com

The author can also be contacted at his website:

charlesray-author.com

Printed in the United States of America

Cover design and photography by the author

Copyright © 2017 Charles Ray

All rights reserved.

ISBN: 1976543495
ISBN-13: 978-1976543494

DEDICATION

This book is dedicated to the muralists and other street artists whose fantastic work make our city and area more beautiful with their amazing work.

The Art of DC's Streets

A lot of DC's street art has been catalogued, and can be seen on various web sites; one has only to use the search phrase 'DC Street Art.' In this volume, I've included a few, including one of the most famous, the mural of DC-native, Marvin Gaye, which is at 7th and S Street, NW, on the wall of a recreation center. Most of the photos here, though, are of less well-known art works, as well as some straight graffiti. I don't give precise of these artworks' locations deliberately—although, most are in the Shaw/Howard University or Cardoza/U Street areas. My hope is that interested readers will bestir themselves to explore the city for themselves, not only to find the works I show here, but to find the thousands of others.

The murals have for the most part been commissioned by the property or business owners as a way to spice up an otherwise dull landscape. You'll not, for instance, that some businesses have murals incorporated into the establishment itself. Others, though, are clearly the independent work of graffiti artists publicly expressing themselves—and, probably in the dead of night when there's no one to impede their artistic inspiration.

Look and enjoy, and hopefully, by the time you reach the end, you'll realize that Washington, DC is not the staid, boring center of government, or the stately monuments, but a lively, vibrant community, rich in diversity and creativity.

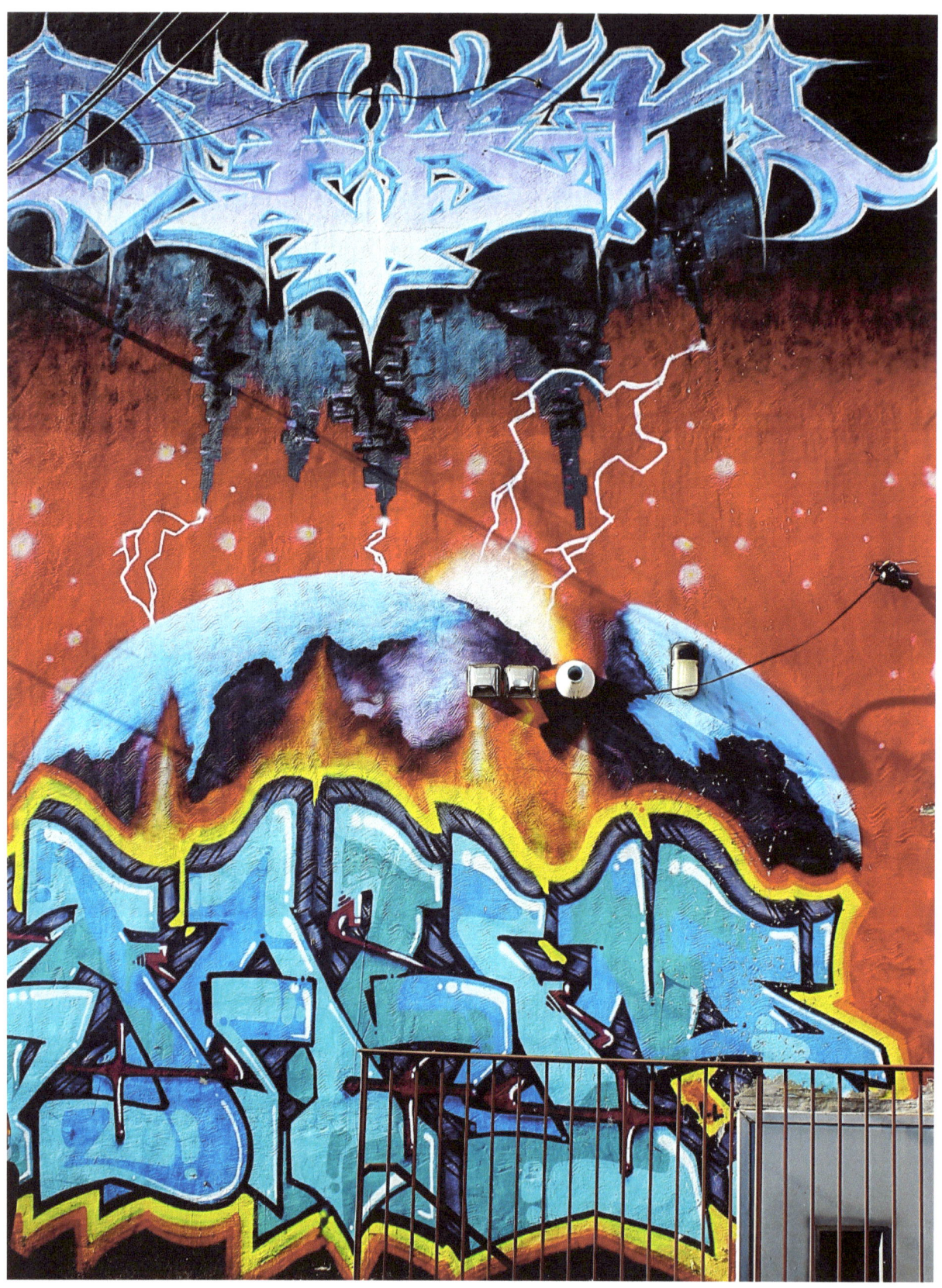

A bright bit of artistic statement on a wall in Shaw District.

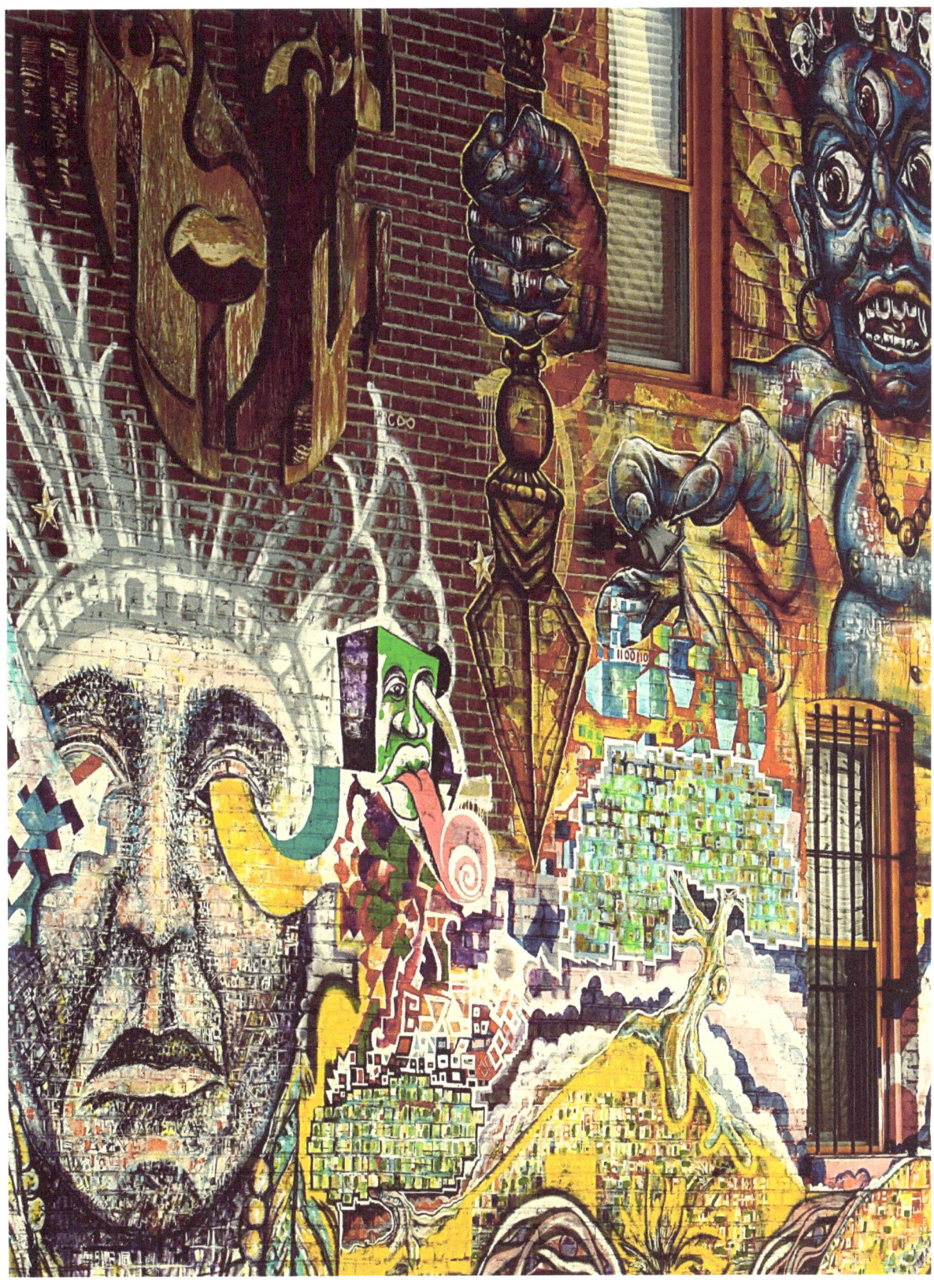

An ornate wall painting in an alley not far from Howard University.

Charles Ray

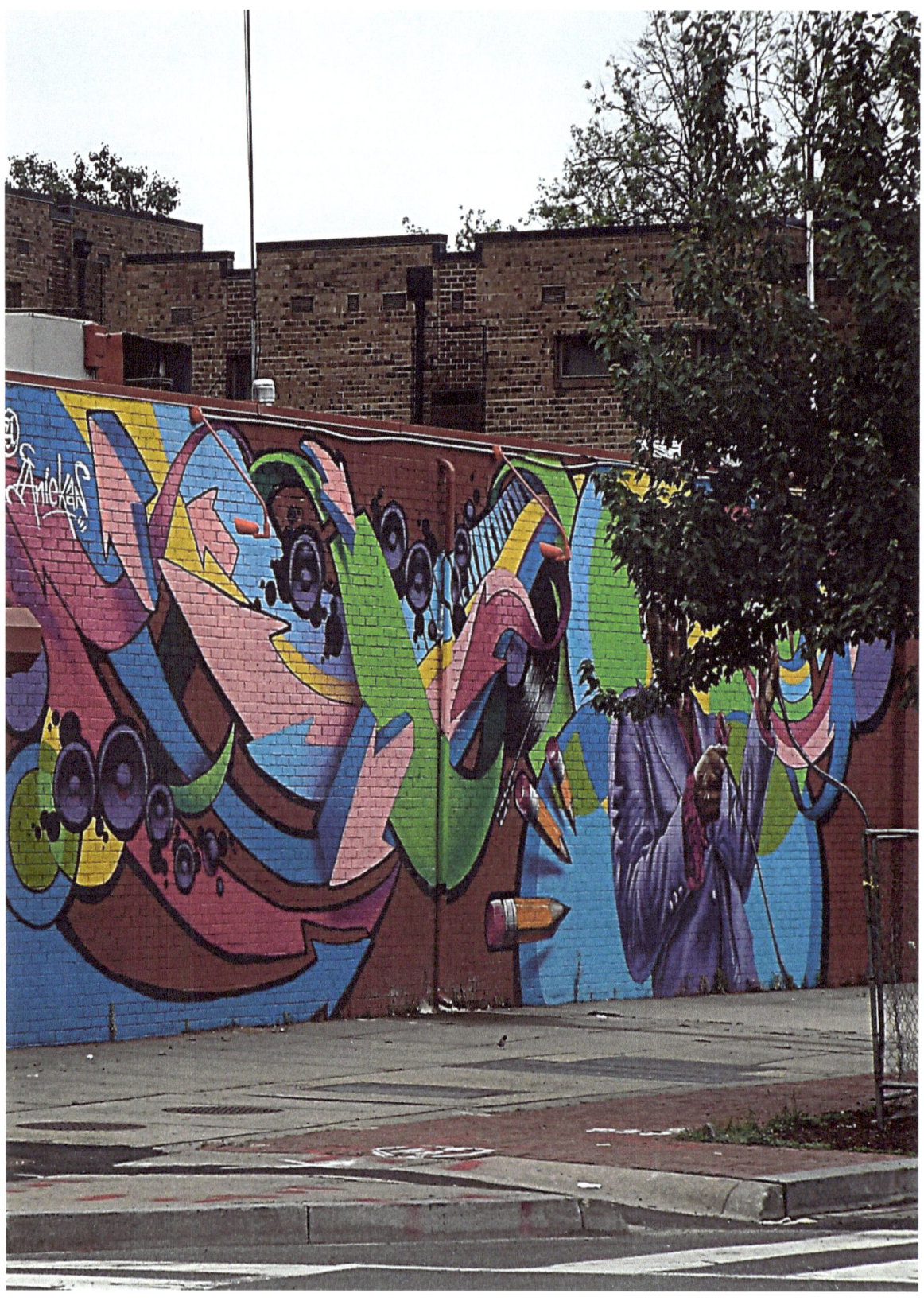

Mural featuring famous DC-resident, Marvin Gaye, on rec center wall.

DC Street Art

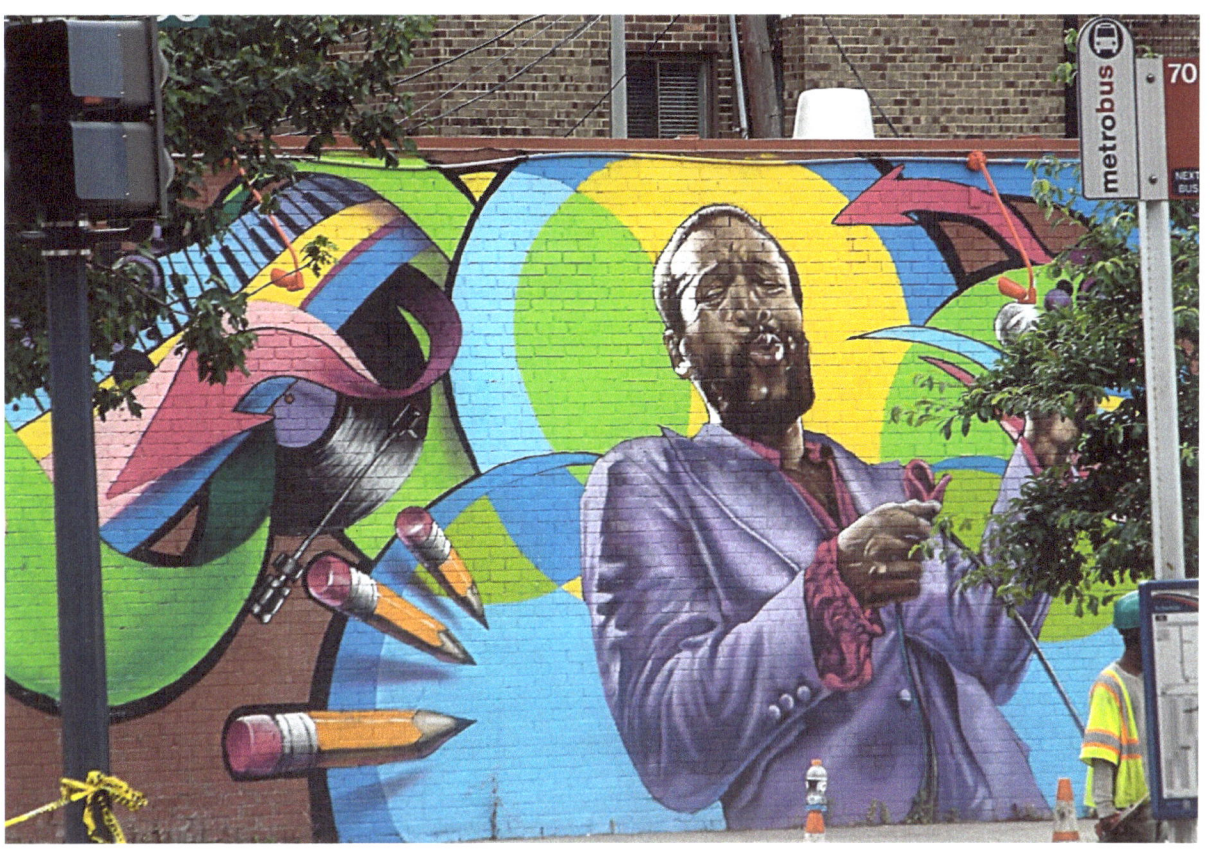

Close-up of the Marvin Gaye mural.

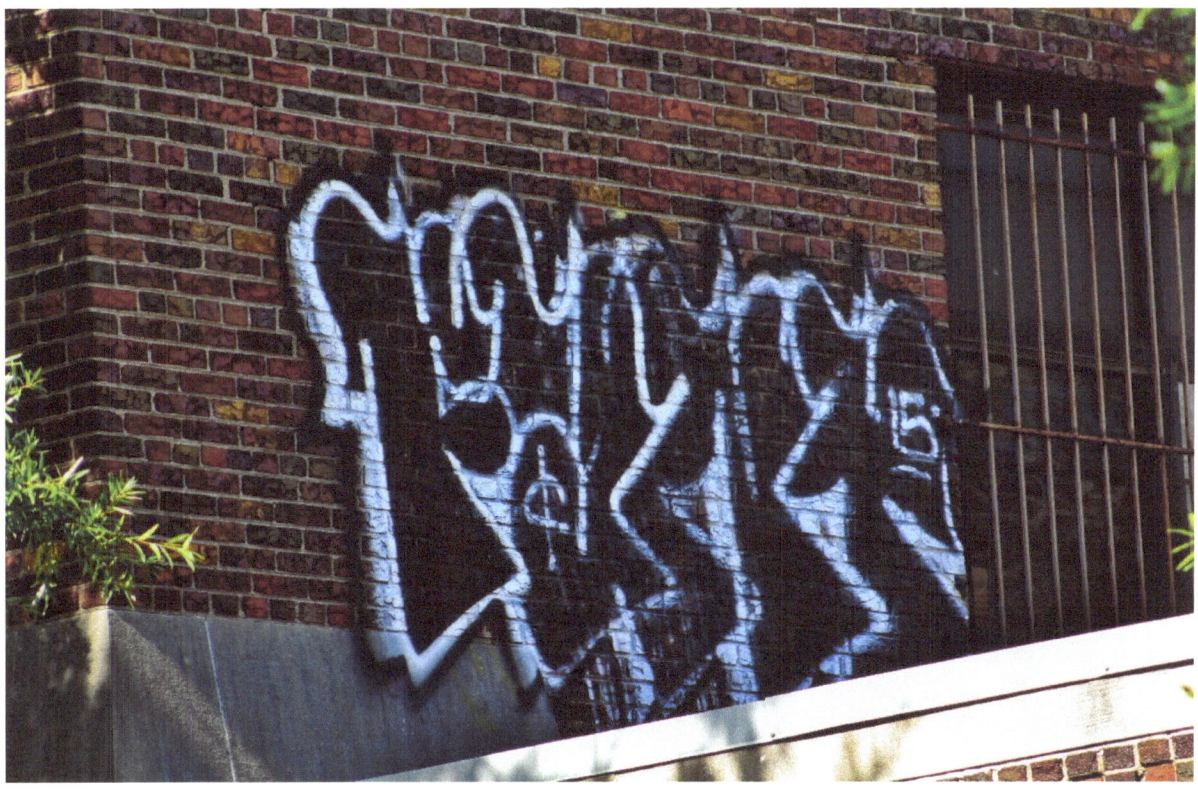

Just a message on a wall.

Charles Ray

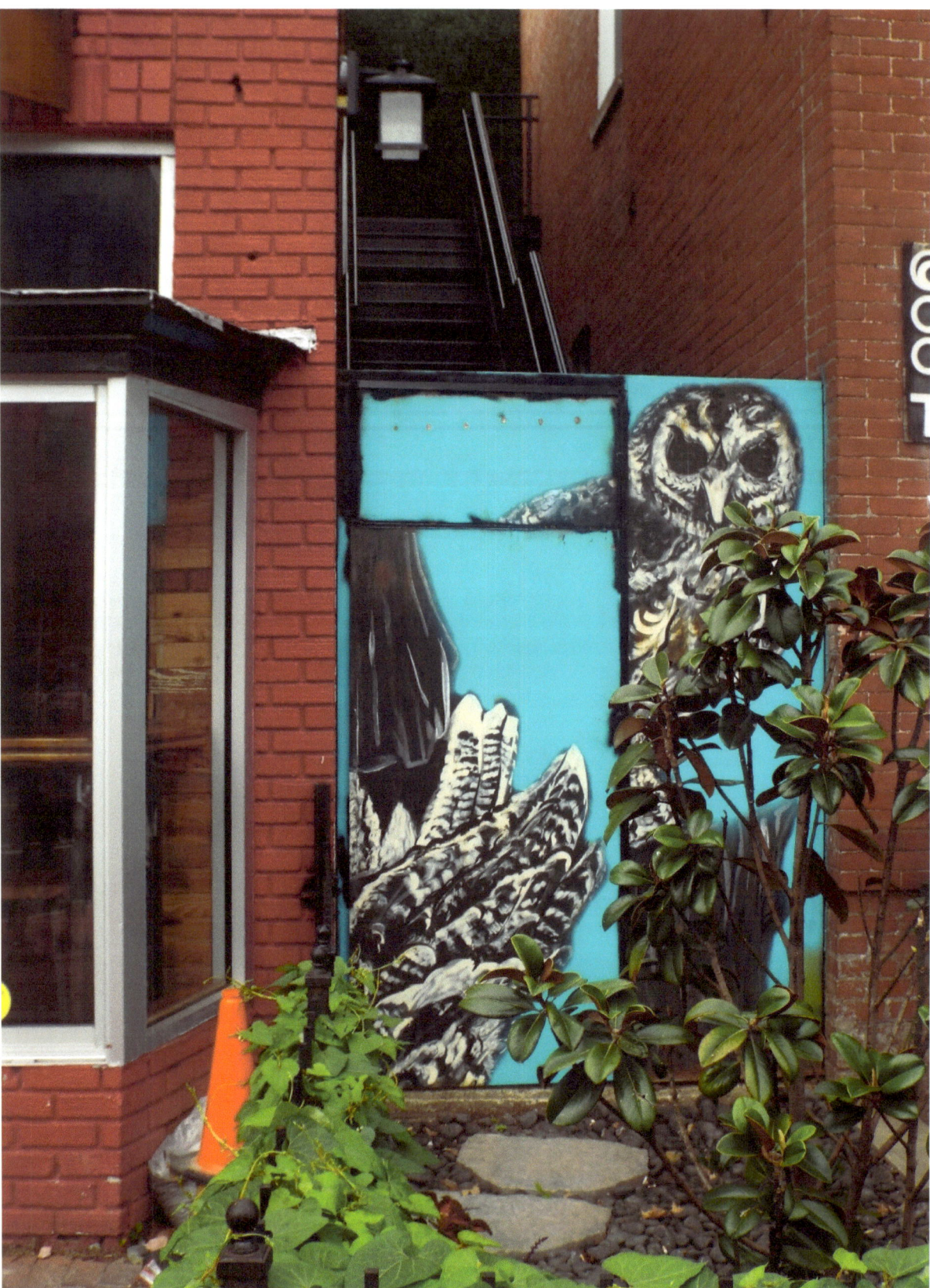

An intricately-painted owl graces this metal door.

DC Street Art

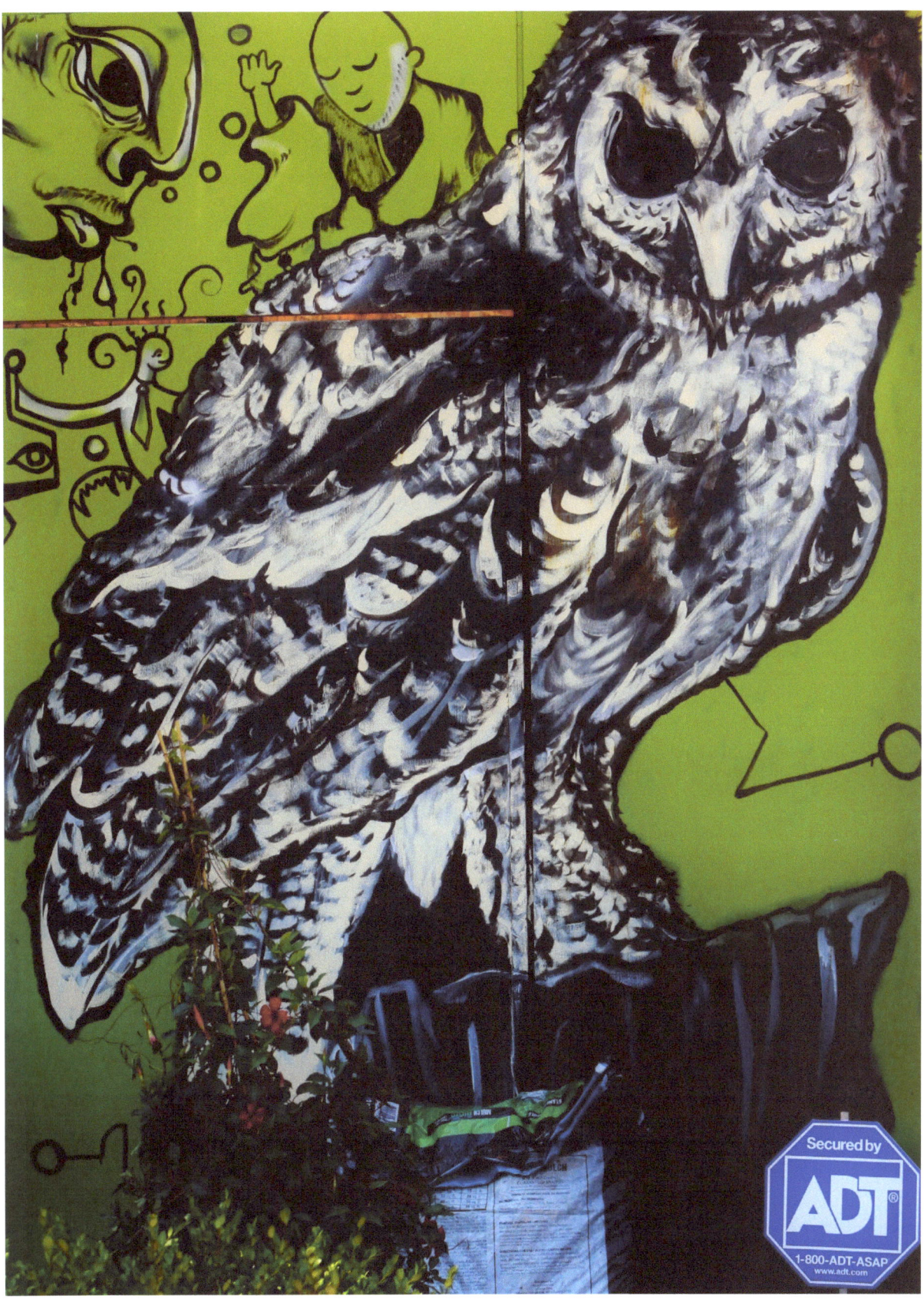

Another owl, obviously by the same artist, also in the Shaw area.

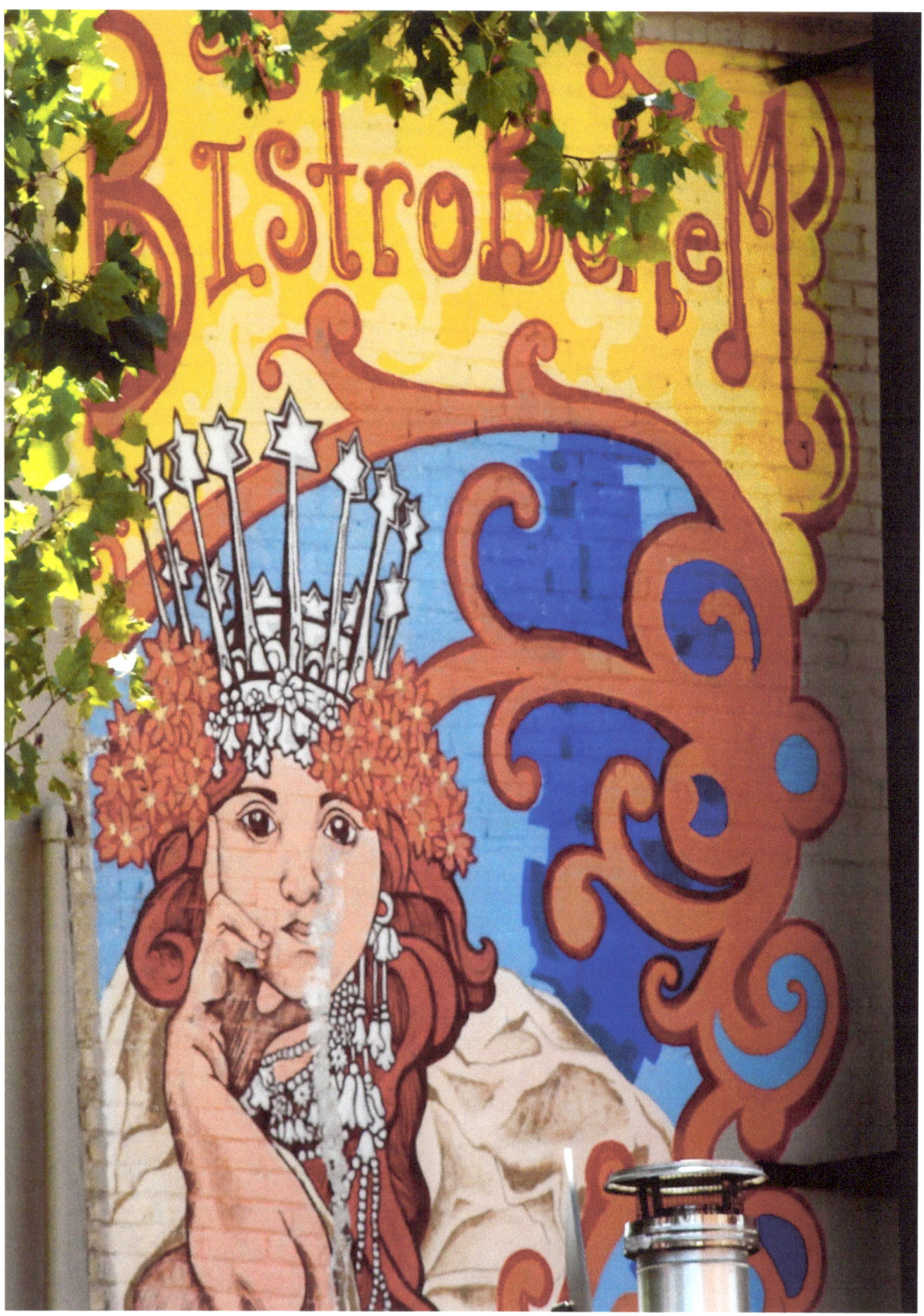

A coffee shop's sign near Duke Ellington Square in Shaw District.

DC Street Art

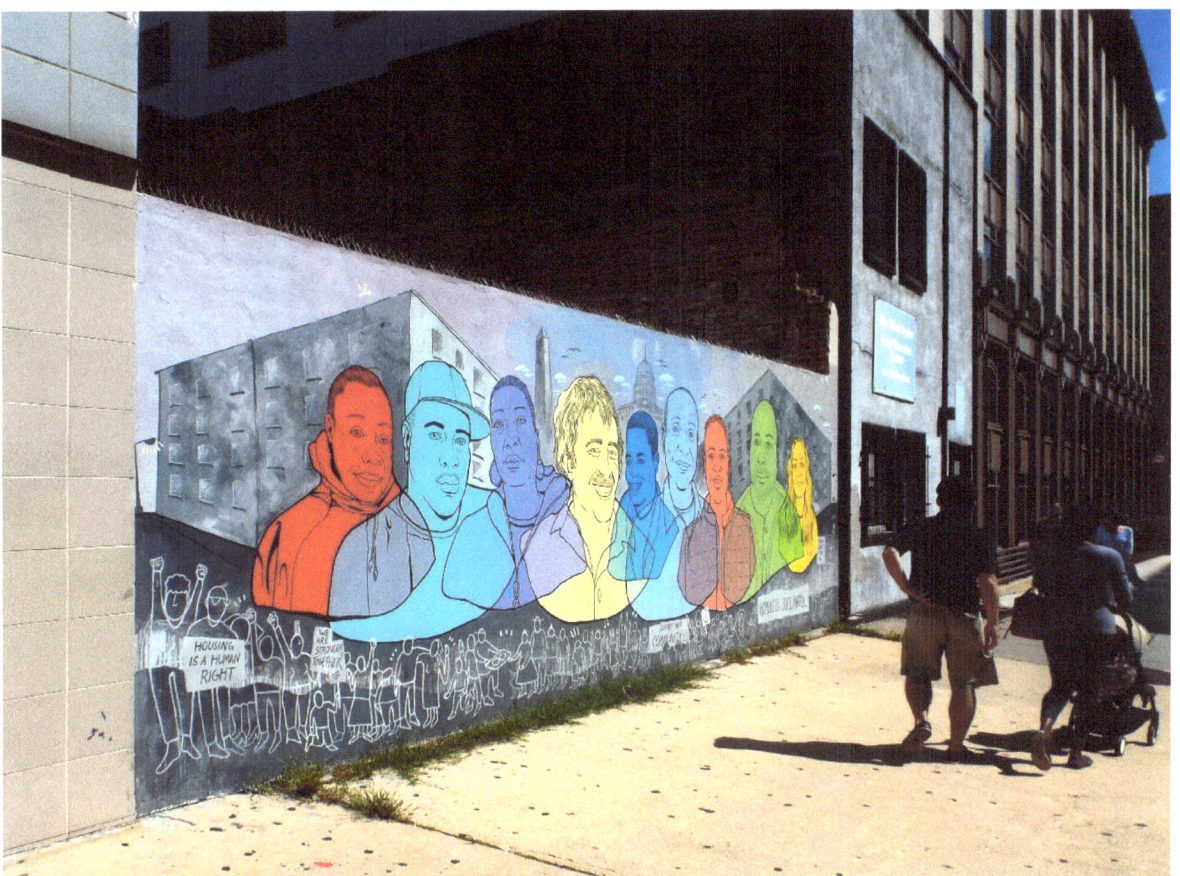

Wall mural near homeless shelter north of Judiciary Square Metro, ignored by tourists.

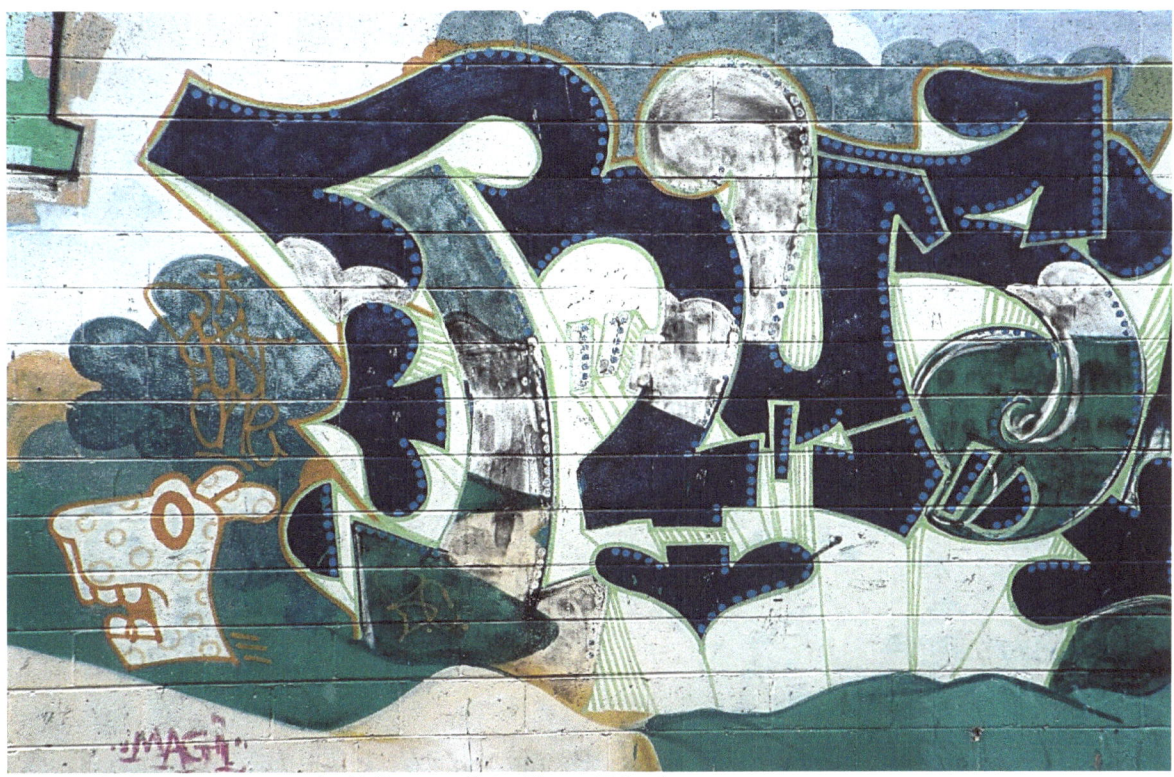

A bit of abstract art on a building wall in Shaw District

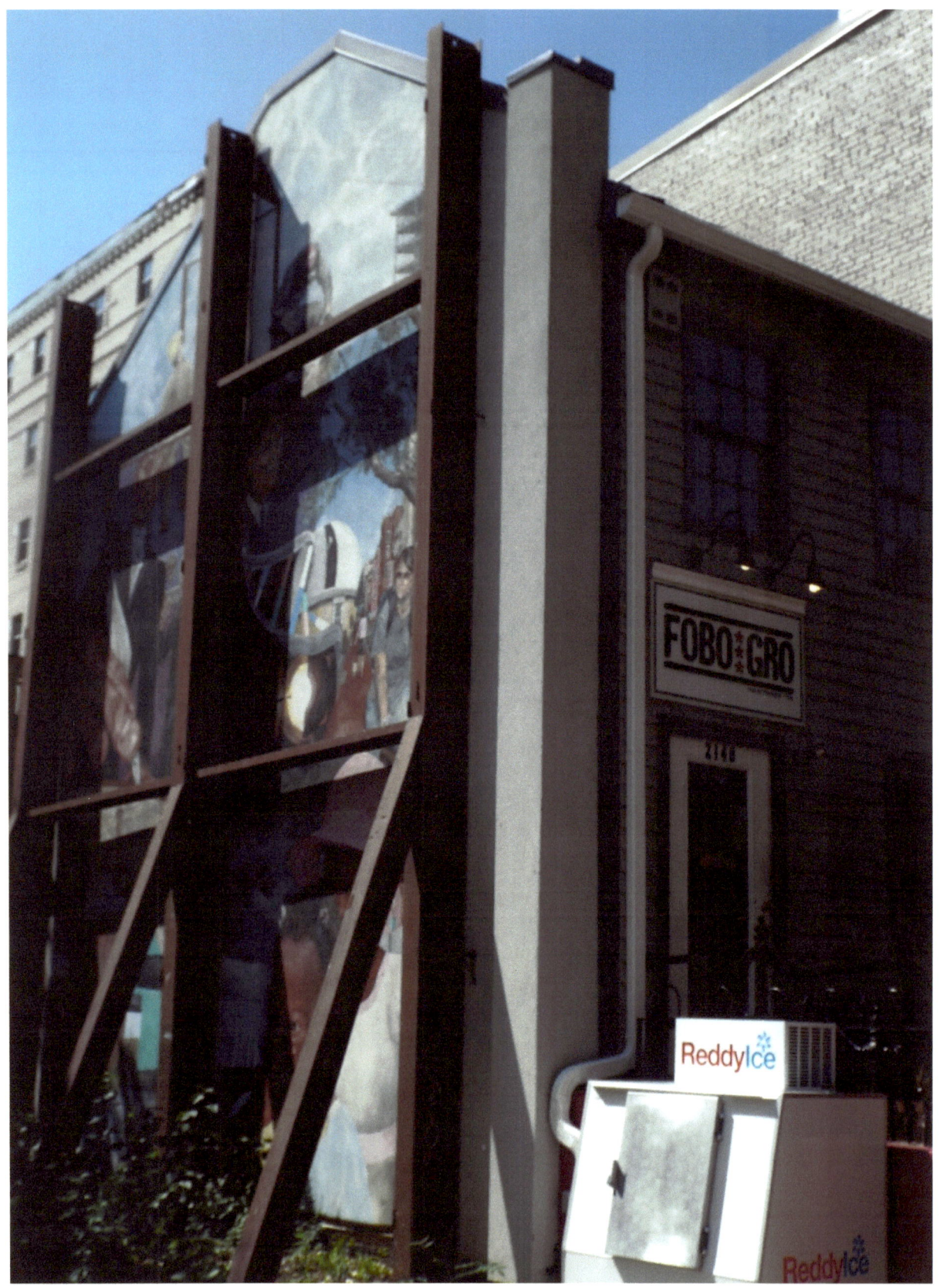

A faded mural on the wall of a small grocery store in Foggy Bottom on the campus of GWU.

DC Street Art

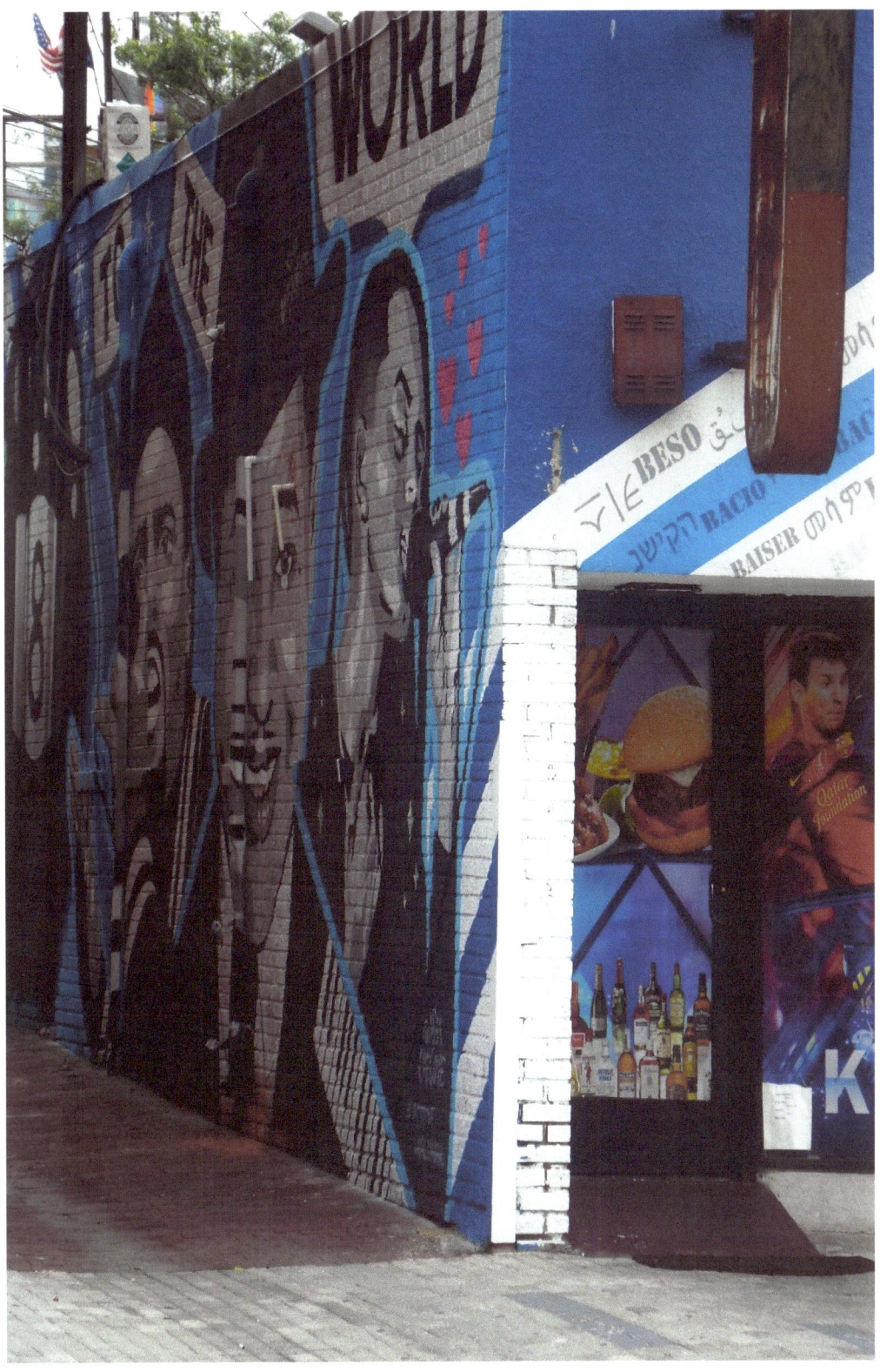

With this store in Shaw District, it's hard to tell where store ends and mural begins.

Charles Ray

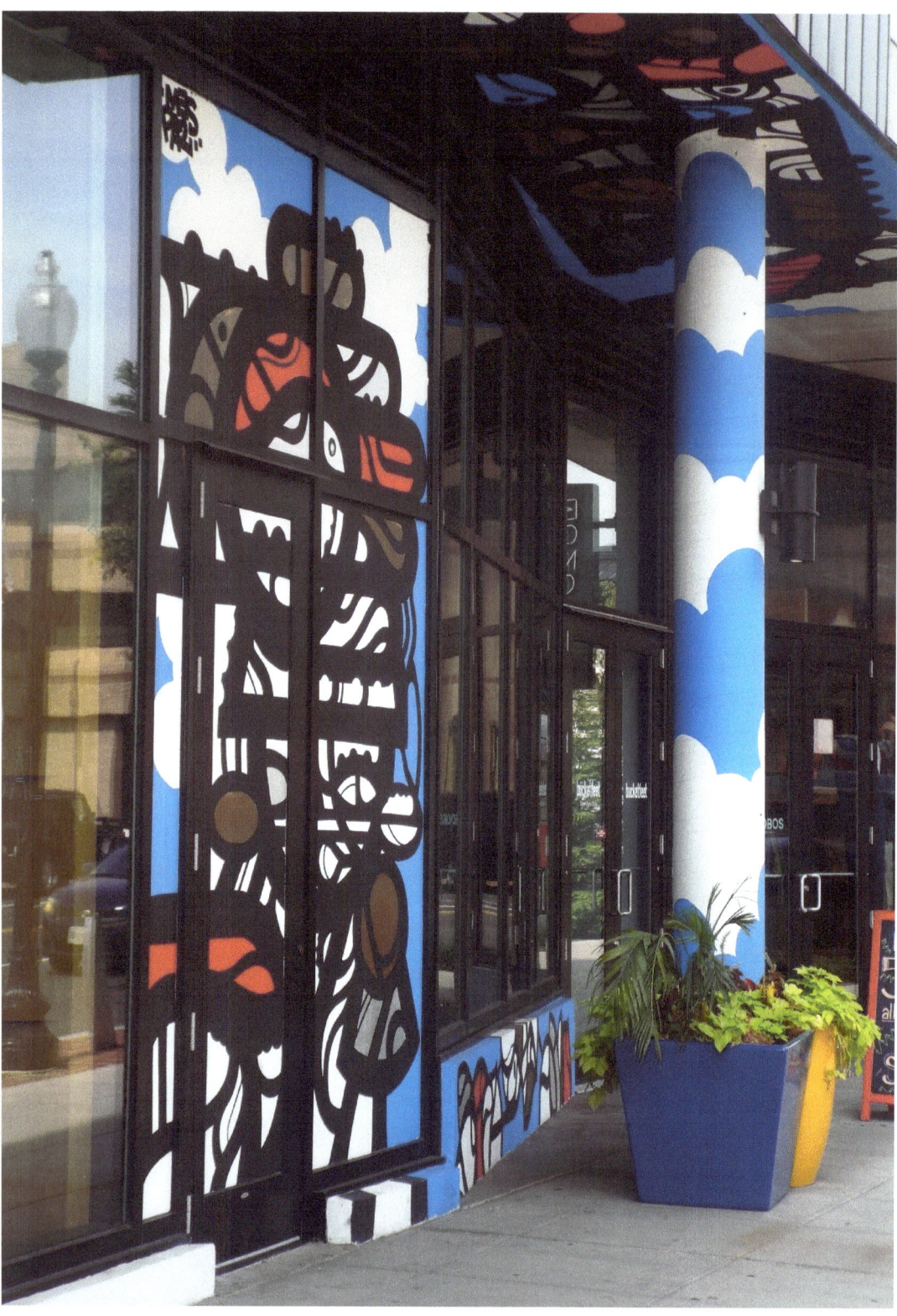

Another Shaw District store that has incorporated street art into it's motif.

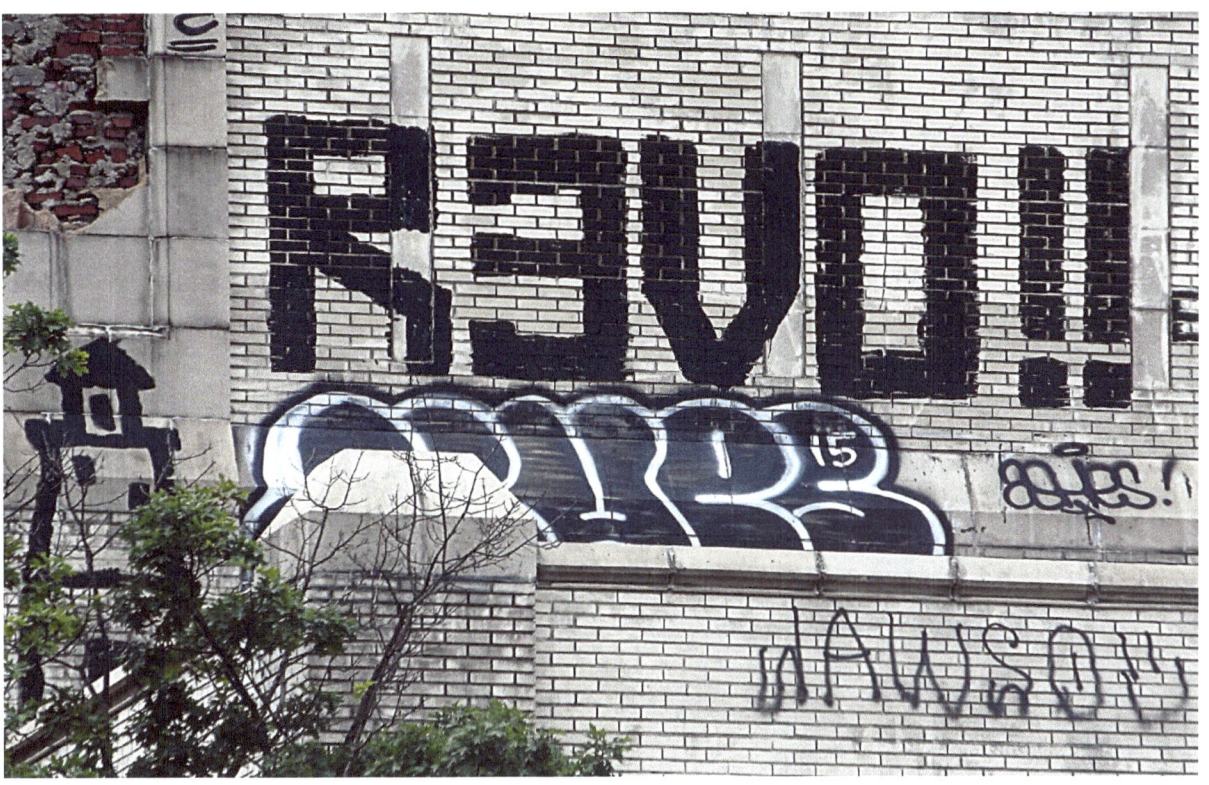

High on a building wall, and in reverse. Quite inventive.

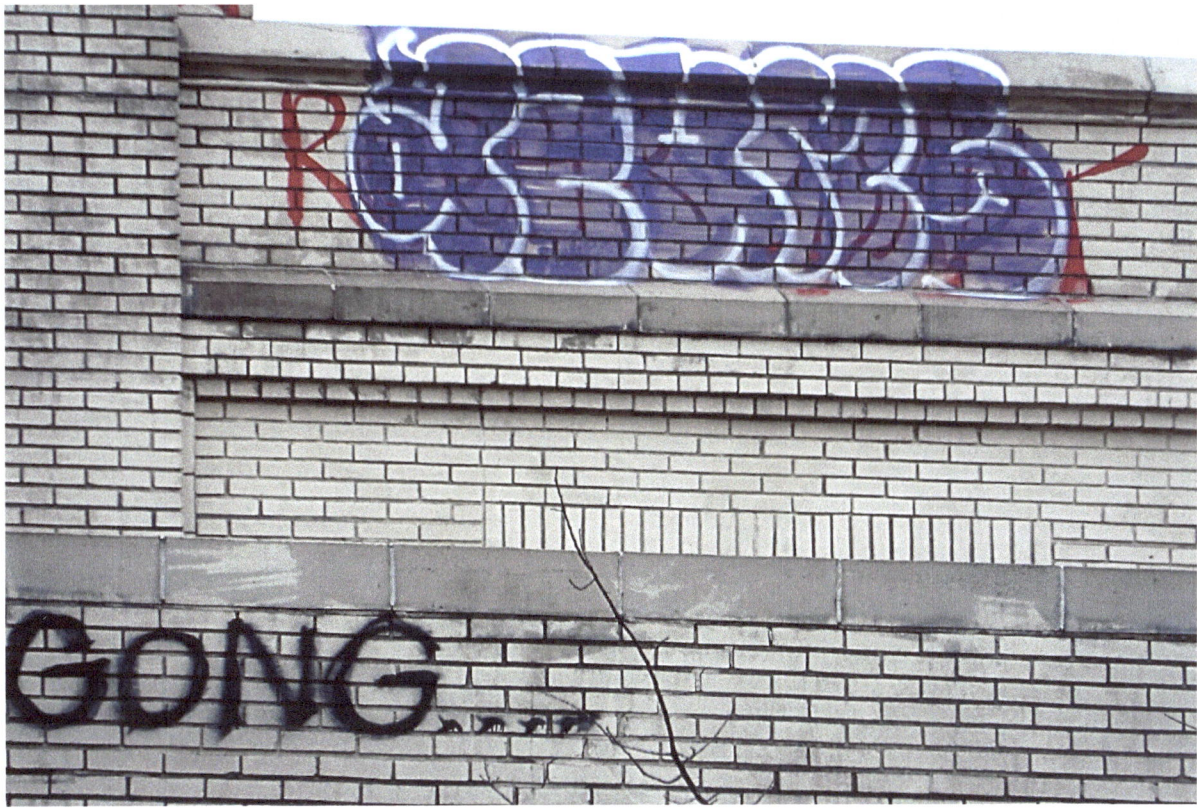

Here, it looks like one artist has painted over the work of another. Same building as above.

Charles Ray

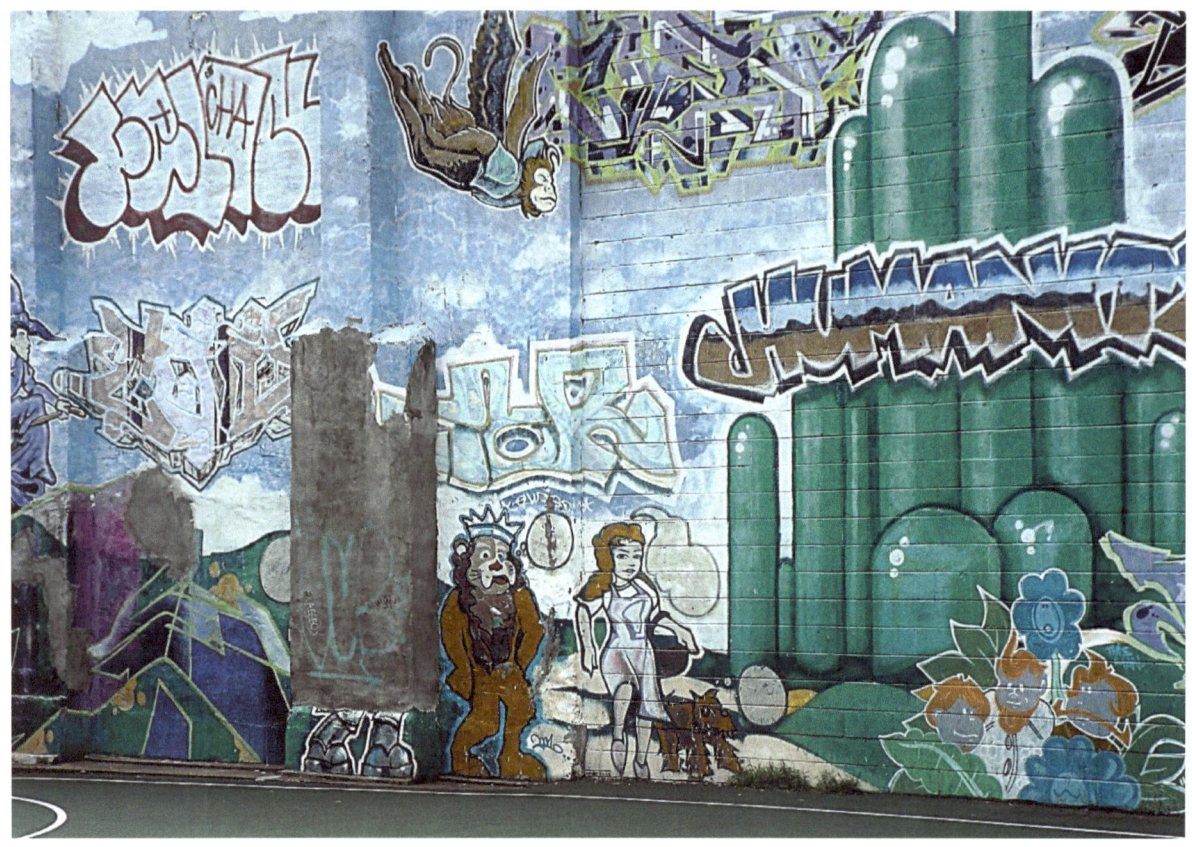

Fairy tale creatures with in an Oriental art style.

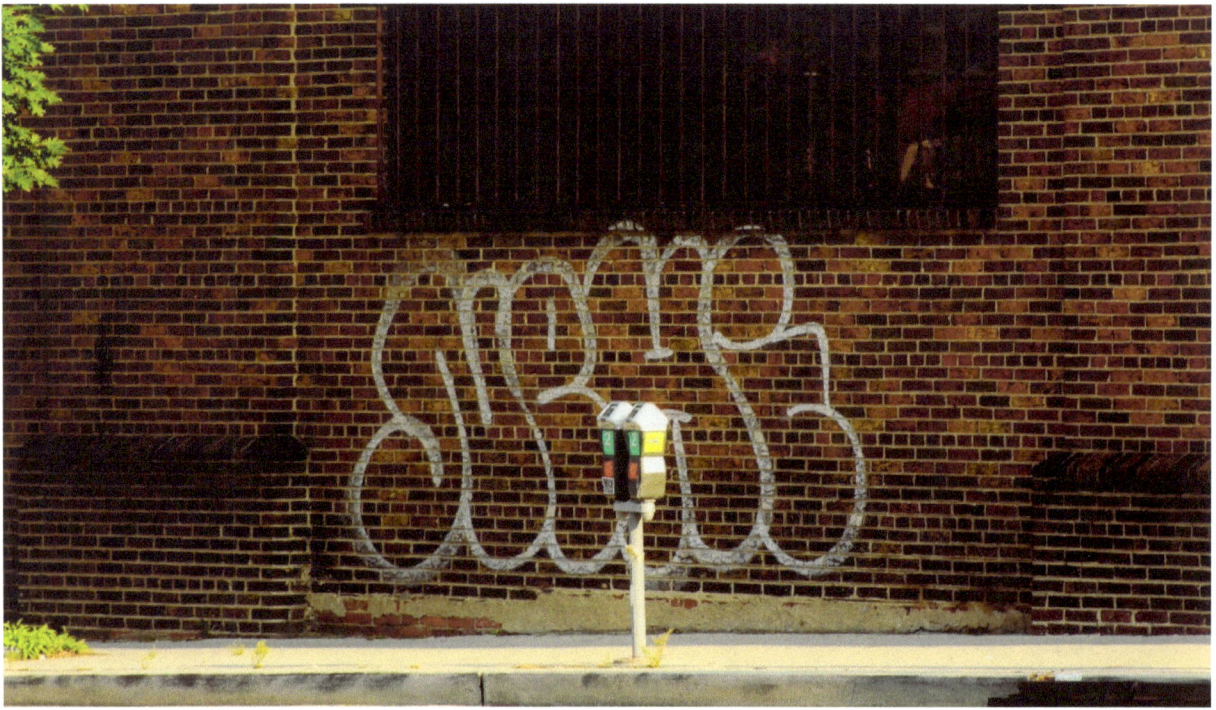

Minimalist art on a wall on Georgia Avenue in Shaw District.

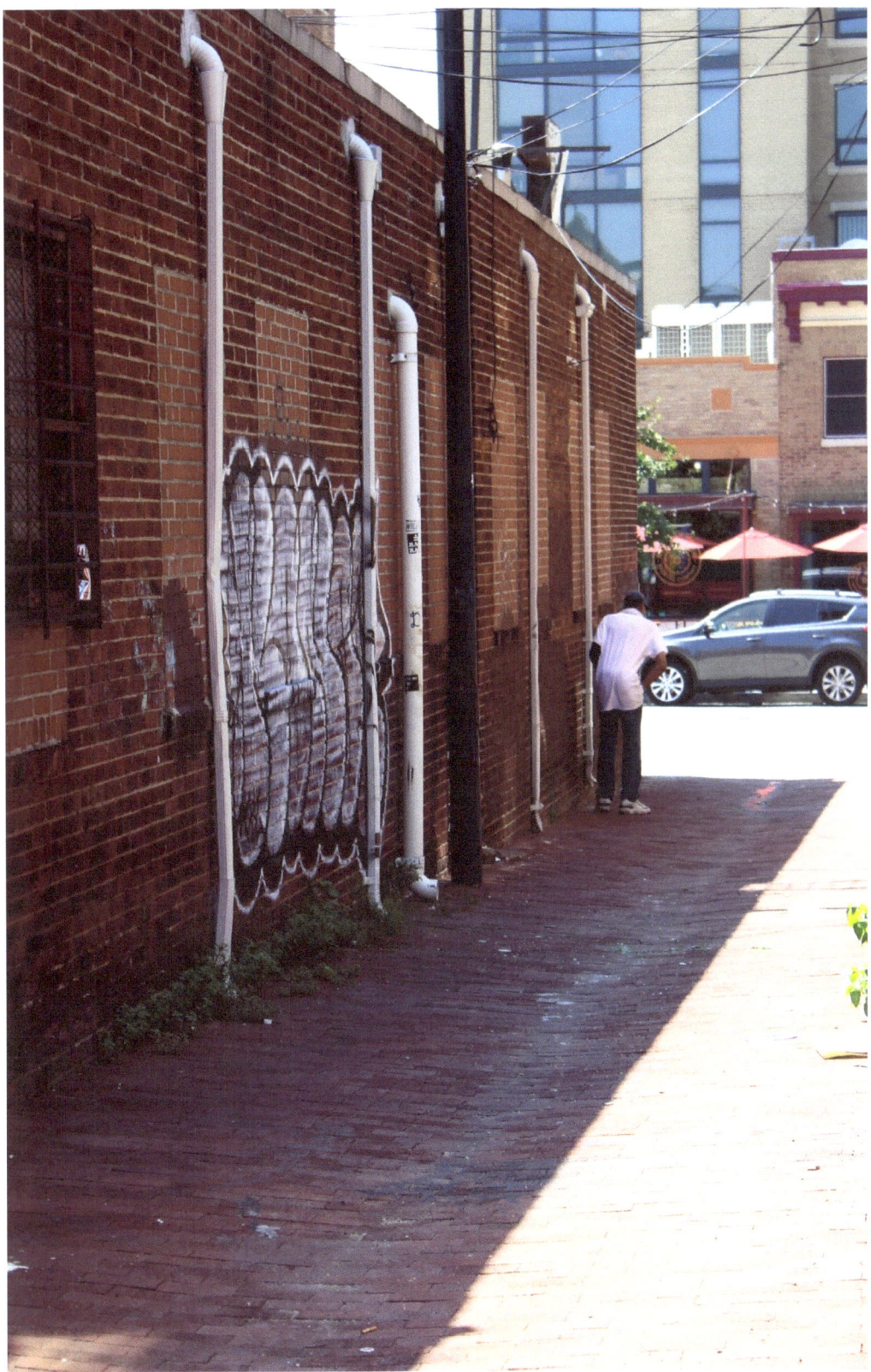

Graffiti on an alley wall near Florida Avenue in Shaw District.

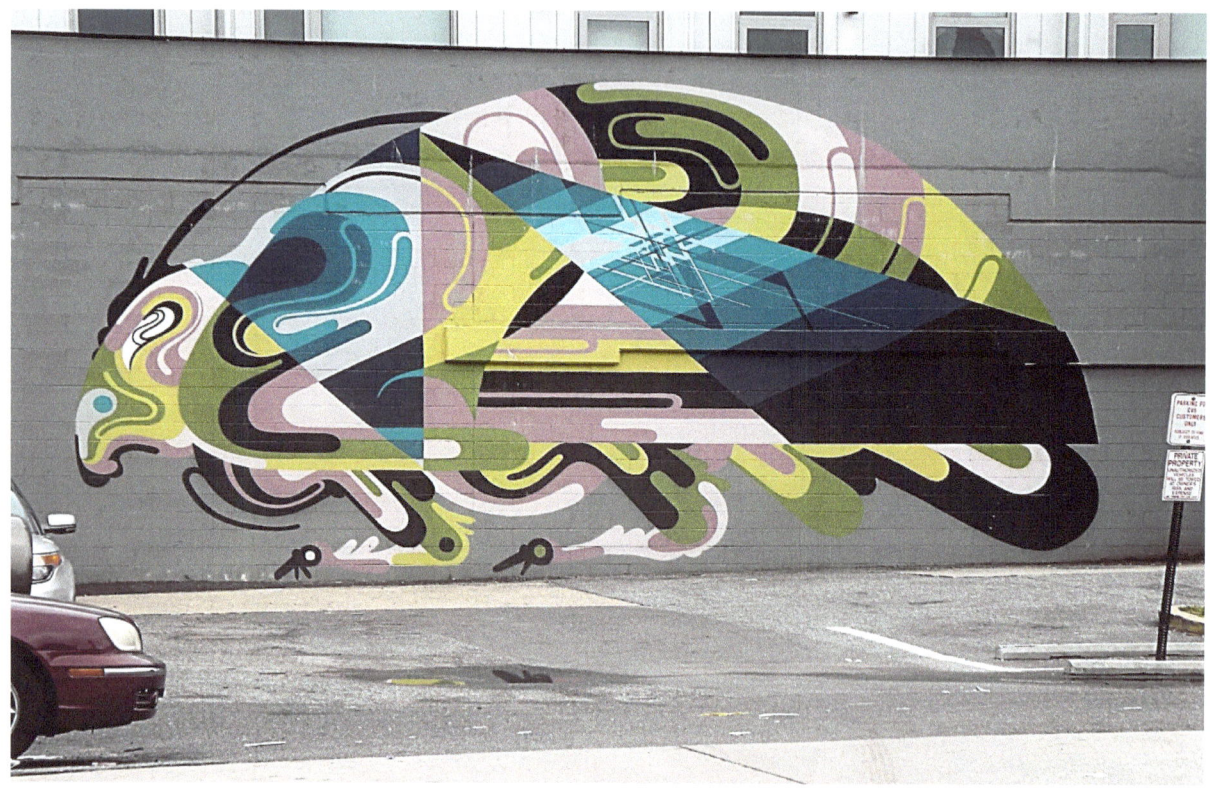

Abstract art on parking lot wall.

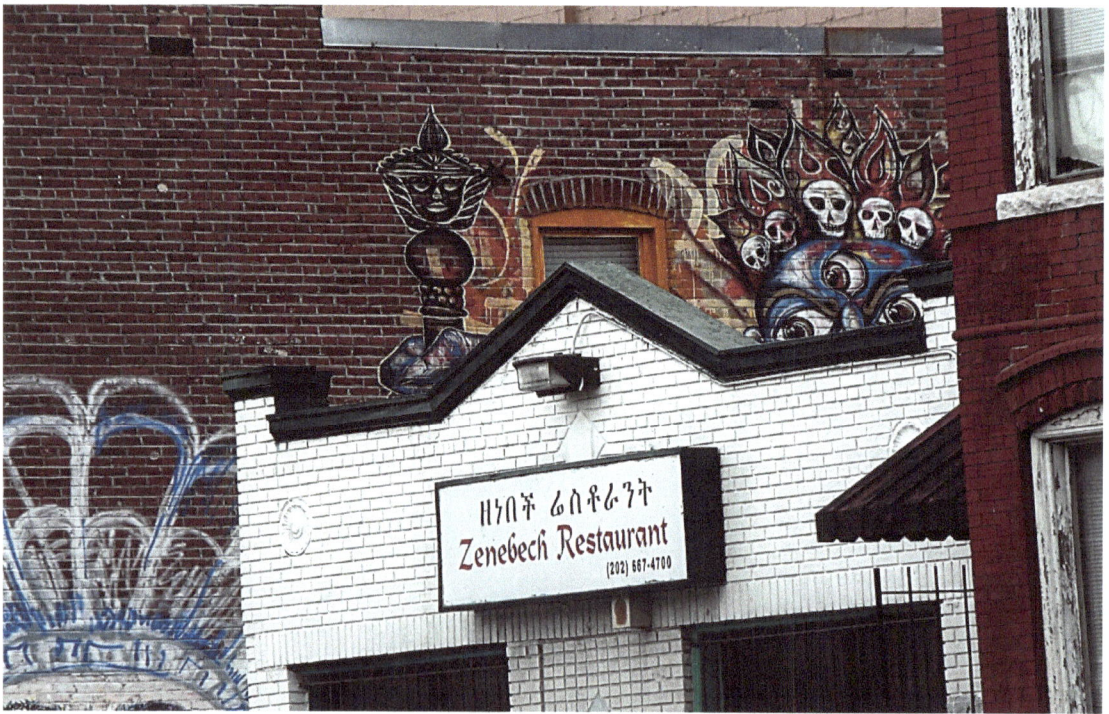

Wall art compliments business, all forming a harmonious whole.

DC Street Art

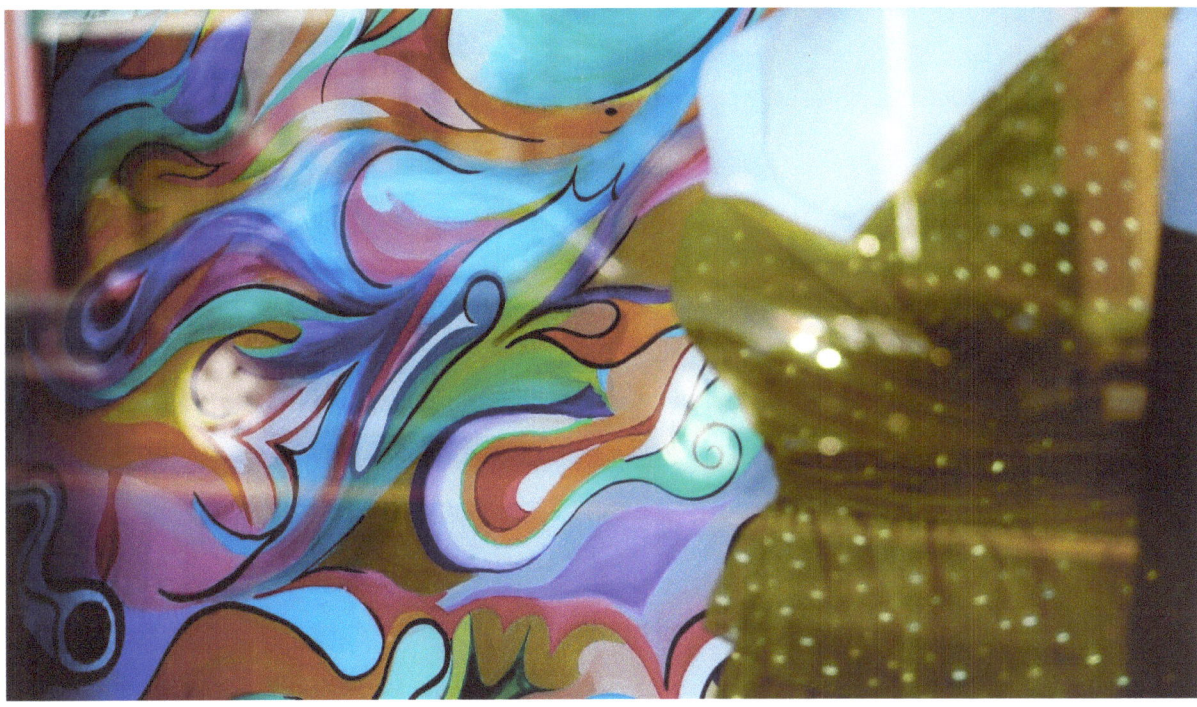

An interesting piece of art incorporated with a store's window display.

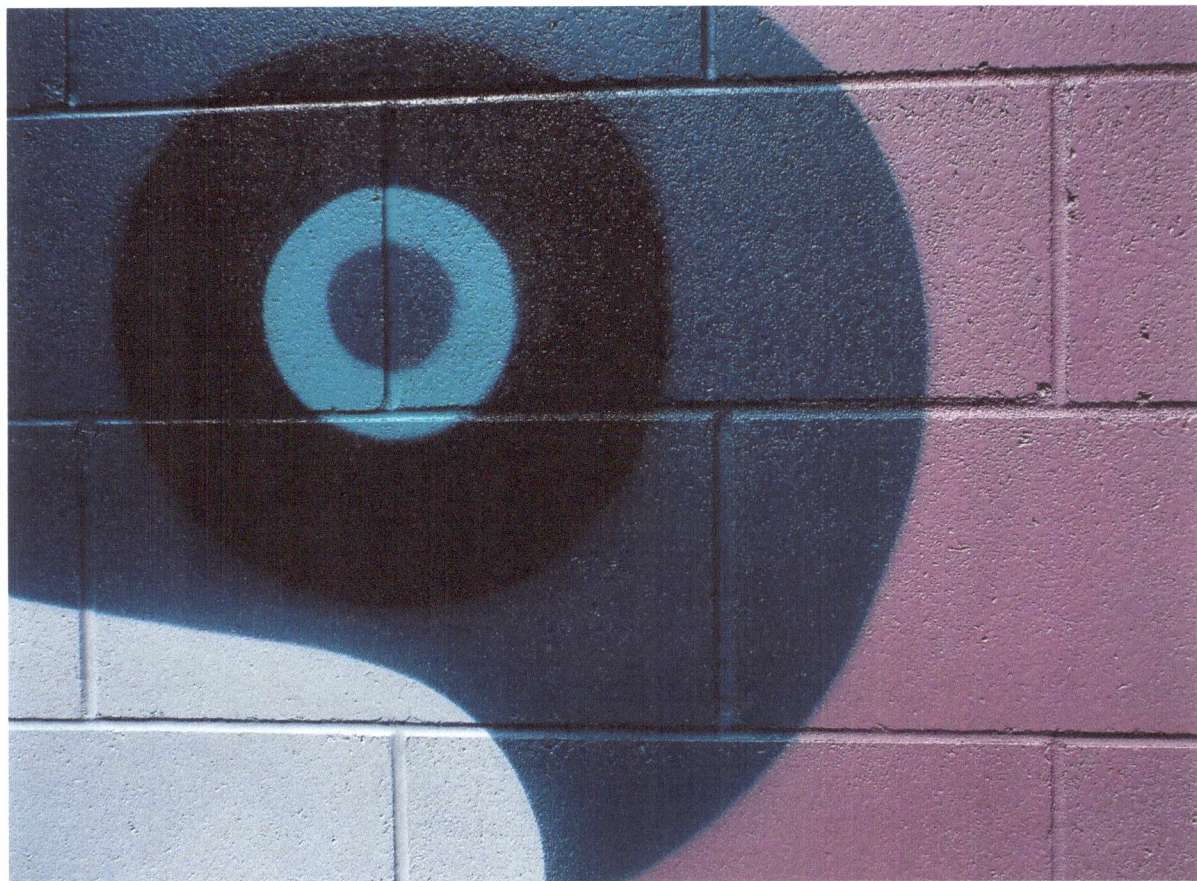

Detail from a mural found in Shaw District.

Charles Ray

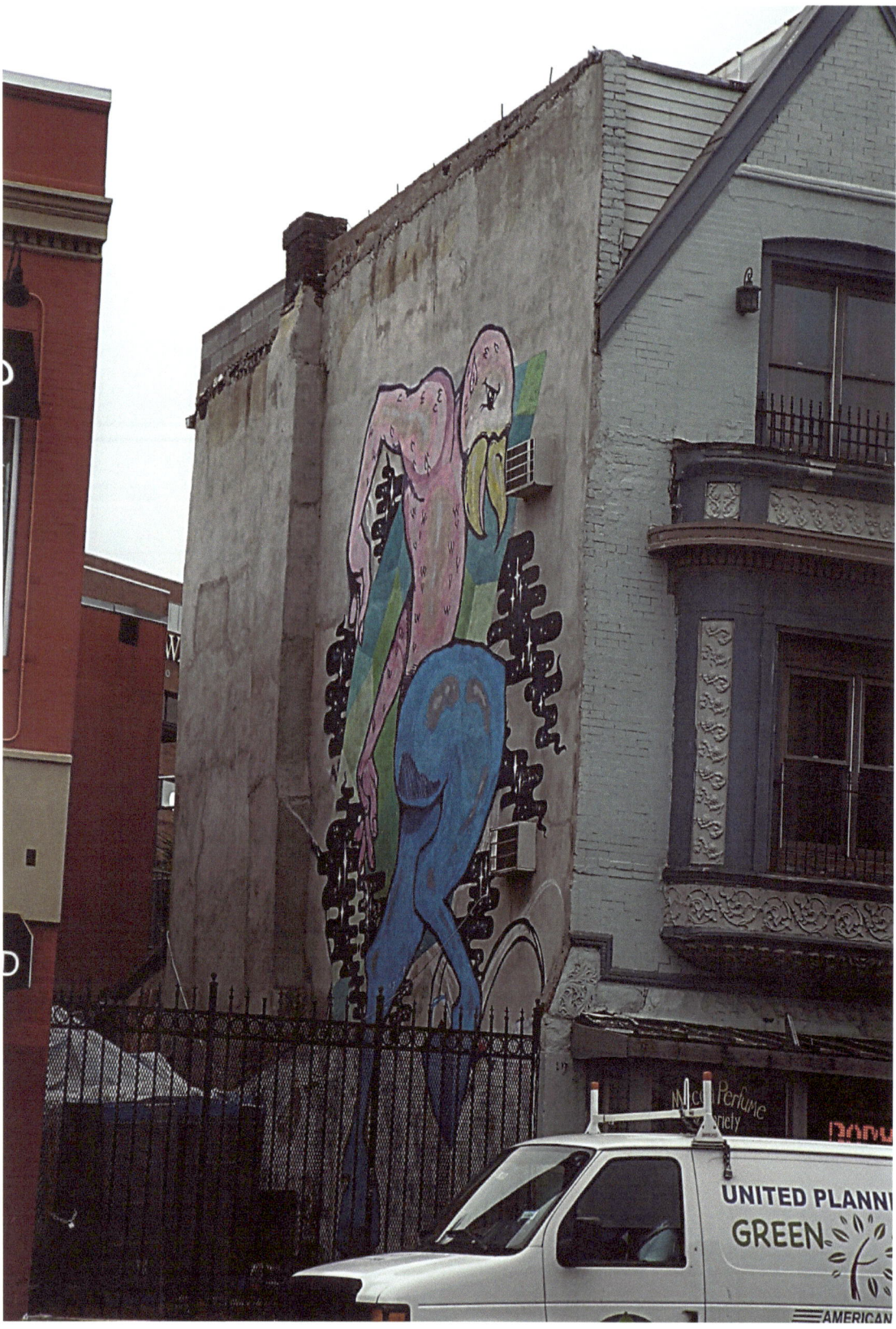

A colorful wall decoration.

DC Street Art

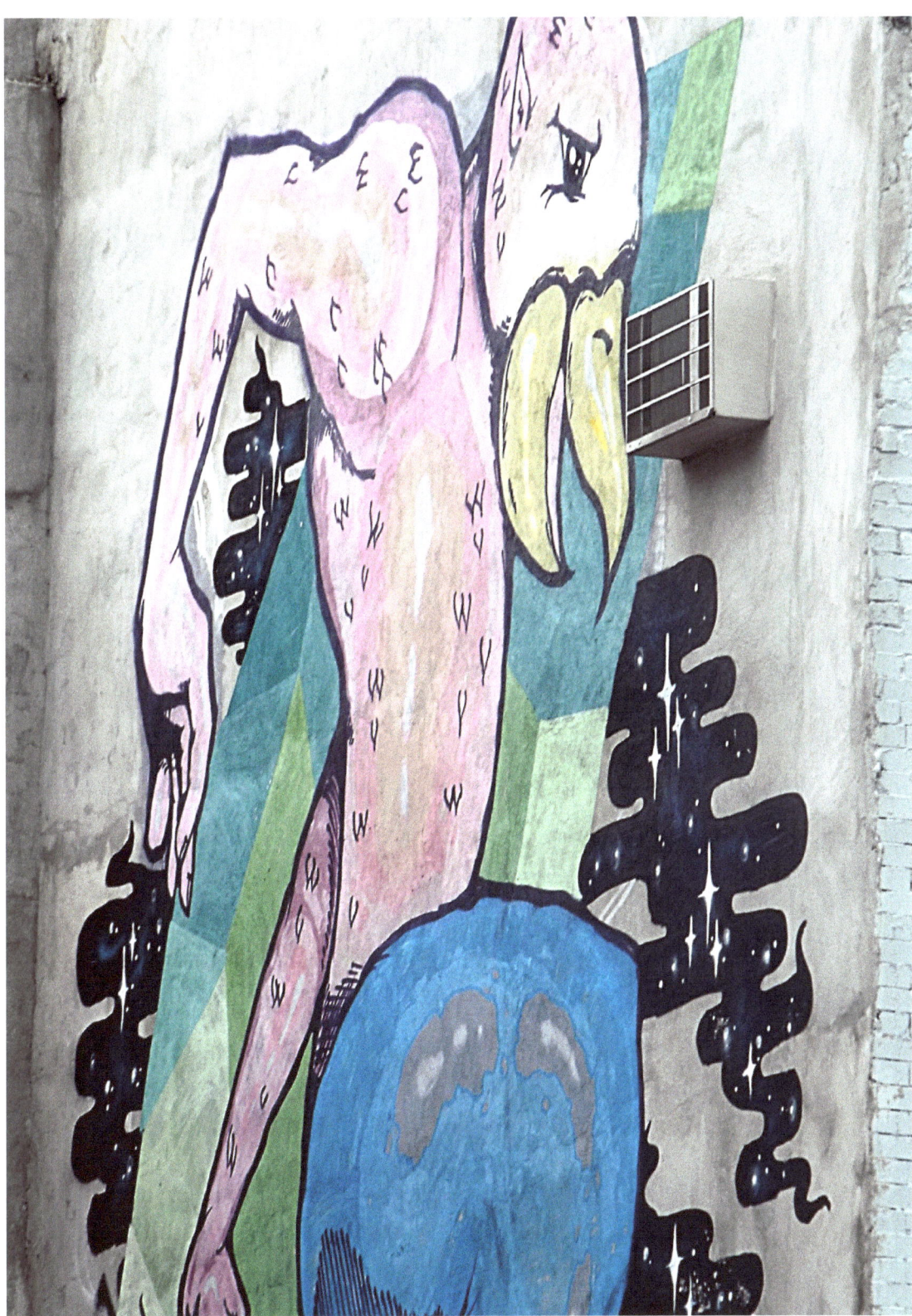

Closeup of the mural.

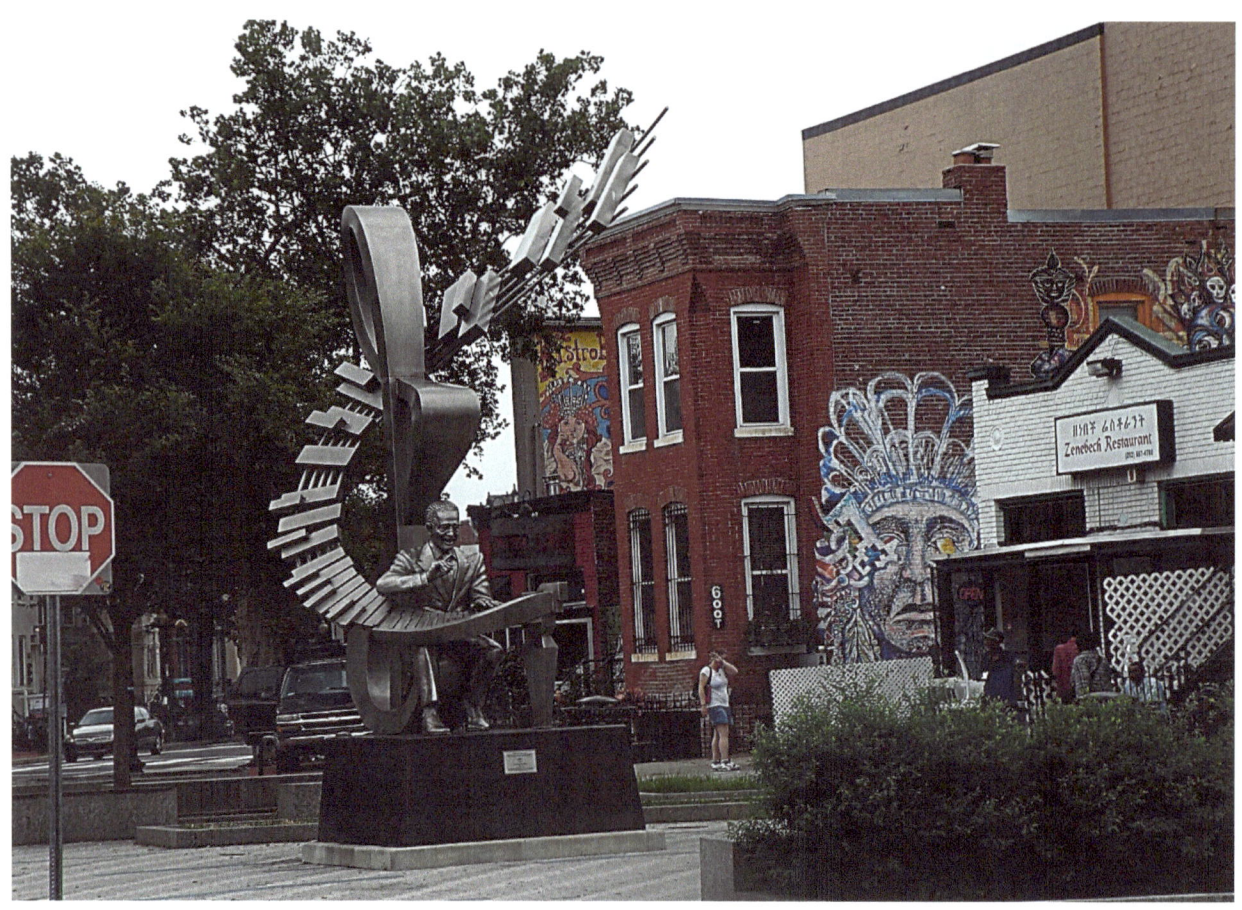

A combination of traditional art and street art in Shaw's Duke Ellington Square.

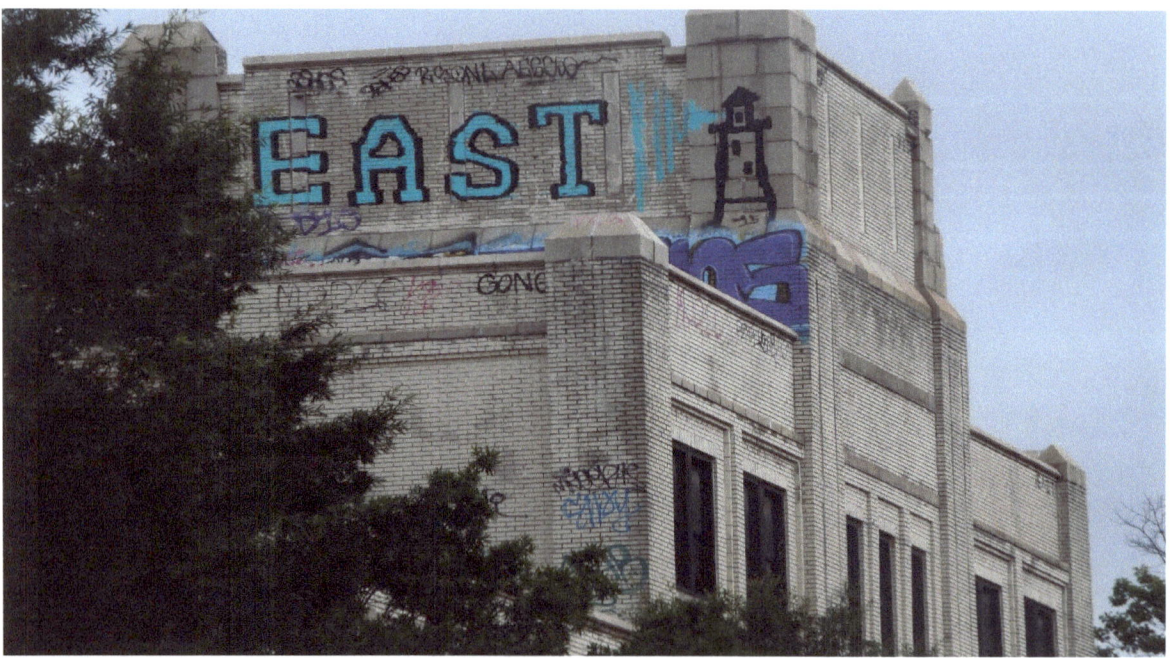

Graffiti artists go to great lengths to tag buildings.

Notes

The photographs contained in this book were taken during the period 2014 to 2017, mainly in the Shaw and Cardoza districts of the capital, although some were taken in Foggy Bottom and other areas. Another area of street art, and one that I did not visit, is the Woodley Park district, not far from the National Zoo.

I have several cameras, digital and film (although I use almost exclusively digital these days), and the one I used for these photos was my FujiFilm FinePix S6800 because of its portability. Post processing, including cropping, color saturation, and contrast adjustment, was done with PhotoScape. The covers were designed with PowerPoint and fonts that were preloaded on Microsoft Office 365.

Charles Ray

ABOUT THE AUTHOR

Charles Ray began his adventure in photography at the age of three when he used his mother's Kodak Brownie camera to snap a selfie—although, that word hadn't been invented in 1948. He didn't get his own camera until 1962, after joining the U.S. Army and being sent to Germany. Since then, though, he has been photographically documenting his travels around the world. In addition to being an avid shutterbug, he's an artist—was once editorial cartoonist for a North Carolina weekly newspaper, and has had art and cartoons published in a number of publications—and writer. First published at the age of 13, when he won a short story contest sponsored by a national Sunday school magazine, he has written for newspapers and magazines in the U.S. and abroad.

He published his first book-length work, an essay on leadership, in 2008, and has since independently published more than 60 works of fiction and nonfiction. Now an independent publisher, he is the author of the Al Pennyback mystery series, the Ed Lazenby cozy mystery series, and the Buffalo Soldier western/history series, as well as the popular *Frontier Justice: Bass Reeves, Deputy U.S. Marshal*. In 2017, he published *Ethical Dilemmas and the Practice of Diplomacy*, an examination of the value-conflict issues facing American diplomats in a time of ethical and moral uncertainty.

Ray has, career-wise, been something of a peripatetic nomad; twenty years in the U.S. Army, thirty years as an American diplomat with the U.S. Foreign Service, and for the past five years, a freelance consultant, author, and lecturer. In 1990, he had a small (uncredited) role in the black comedy, *Air America*, as a dispatcher for the CIA's covert airline in Southeast Asia, and has appeared in a number of documentaries over the years.

A native of Texas, since retiring from government service in 2012, he has made his home in suburban Maryland, just outside Washington, DC, and spend a lot of his time studying and documenting the history of some of the lesser-known aspects of the area.

www.ingramcontent.com/pod-product-compliance
Lightning Source LLC
Chambersburg PA
CBHW040057250526
45473CB00043B/1817